T0145166

A Taste of Sadi

SEYYIDA WESTBROOK
PHOTOGRAPHY: TONY KIGANO

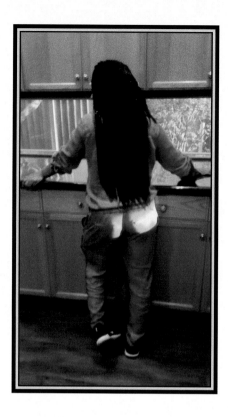

To order additional copies of this book, contact:
Xlibris
844-714-8691
www.Xlibris.com
Orders@Xlibris.com

ISBN: Softcover   978-1-6641-8996-6
        Hardcover   978-1-6641-8997-3
        EBook   978-1-6641-8995-9

Library of Congress Control Number: 2021917193

Print information available on the last page.

Rev. date: 08/24/2021

Dedication

Aaron, Destiny and Shavonce this book is dedicated to you. Have no fear of perfection, always aim high and know that god will be there every step of the way to catch you. Live your passion, pray have faith and be patient and kind. Know that family is important, there's nothing more fitting than having a well cooked meal with love ones. Hopefully you find this book useful. Mommy.......

Introduction

When I think of cooking, I think of the way it makes me feel. That therapeutic feeling, love, life, enjoyment and well- being. That make you want to dance and sing. Looking at life in a different prospective in a higher power. Appreciating God for his grace, mercy and blessings that he has bestowed upon us. And let's not forget about all the miracles God preformed. Such as, the five thousand people fed with only five loaves of bread and two fish. The more I think about our sweet savior, the more I want to imitate him feeding and sharing my cook book viral around the world is a big deal for me. With each bit of my meal would transform a frown into a smile with my chief creativity and hands. As a child growing up, in remembrance and inspired by my mother "Jackie Fields" in the kitchen cooking up receipts my grandmother taught her, that was later passed on to me. Has taught me to follow the great structures that was planted within me. I was told from my mother, as a toddler. How she would continuously have me in the back seat of her car as she would drive around looking for homeless people to feed, with the millions of questions I would ask out of curiosity as I got older until I got complete understanding. A continuously foundation That I know have with my three children. Aaron is my oldest son my first love, who is now 18 years of age. My second child, who happens to be my only girl is 16 years of age. And my last child is my youngest son Shavonce, my five-year-old. Baby of the bunch. Having children comes along with the benefit of molding them just the way you want, with an over flow of love, serenity, time, and of course prayer. Watching my children actions, going on outings or laboring for the lord. Has shown me the compassion they have for others. Reaching in their pockets with their own earnings and soft-spoken words. Evening going as far as Reminding me of being a day late prepping a meal for the homeless. Giving me an unexplainable blessed feeling as a parent, that my children are on the right path. There's no greater feeling than watching a grateful smile with a hot cooked meal. Some people say you never know, you may just be entertaining an angle. But I say, were all angles.

When I get my kitchen, I feel like I'm in a whole other world. My love is often shown not only from my personality and kind words but through my passion. having family and friends over with a hot cooked meal, making sure there happy and full. I refuse to let anyone go home on an empty stomach. Out of my mother's three children, I have always been the oddball different on every level. As far as watching and helping my mother cook, to nurturing, and dancing boldly. Nothing is greater than living your passion. Waking up every day with purpose and joy, ready to conquer the world. My philosophy is, if you don't conquer your passion, you commit spiritual suicide. Always wondering and watching others live your dream.

Taco's

Ingredients

one bag of cheese

box of shell

1 pound of ground beef

one can of black olives

one pack of sharp cheddar cheese

one in and half lettuce

sudais tomato 2 dice tomato

container of sour cream

jar of salsa

one can of tomato paste

so pack of Taco seasoning 2 packs of Taco seasoning

3 teaspoons of garlic powder

3 teaspoons of garlic salt

3 teaspoons of season salt

Direction

Heat stove to high place large skillet on stove. apply ground beef, 3 tea spoons of garlic powder, 3 teaspoons of garlic salt, 3 teaspoons of season salt, continuously stir Ground beef for 15 min. Drain me Add tomato pasta sauce and taco seasoning. Pour all of the olive juice from the can into ground beef for flavor, stir for 5 minutes turn off heat. Cook shells for 6 minutes, Remove from oven. Add 4 teaspoon Taco meat to the shell, one at a time. Add lettuce, 2 teaspoons of sour cream, 1 spoon of chopped olives, 2 tea spoons of diced tomato. 3 teaspoons of salsa, 2 tea spoons of cheese and serve hot.

Creamy Sea Food French Fries

Ingredients

one bag of frozen fries

one stick of butter

1 pound of shrimp

one bag of frozen domestic lump crab

one jar of work bertolli creamy basil Alfredo pasta

squeeze Of teriyaki sauce

¾ of cheddar Jack cheese

½ of sprinkled parmesan cheese

1 tea spoon of garlic powder

1 tea spoon of garlic salt

1 tea soon of season salt

1 spoon of Cheyenne pepper

Directions

bake frozen bag of fries in oven for about 20 minutes, after 10 minutes of baking fries place clean devein large shrimp into skillet add stick of butter garlic powder garlic salt seasoning salt cayenne pepper and a squeeze of teriyaki sauce stir continuously for 4 Minute until turn pink. turn off heat and remove skillet. Pour 1 ¼ of bartelli creamy basil Alfredo sauce into skillet give it a quick stir .pour over fries sprinkle crab meat on top. Apply parmesan cheese and serve hot.

Oatmeal Morning Blast Shake

Ingredients

1 handful of ice

one Cup of oatmeal

one banana

1/2 of blueberry

2 teaspoons of peanut butter

1 ¾ Glass of milk

1 tea spoon of raw honey

Directions

in a blender at raw oatmeal, add raw oatmeal, ice, Whole banana, One handful of blueberries, Peanut butter, milk, Honey, blend on high until very smooth. Pour into glass and drink it right away

Chicken Wings

Ingredients

2 Table Spoons of Corn Starch

1 ½ Cup Of Flour

4 Tea Spoons Of Coconut Flour

1 Tea Spoon Of Garlic Salt

1 Tea Spoon Of Season Salt

1 Tea Spoon Of Black Pepper

½ Hot Sauce

1 Cup Of Pineapple Juice

Directions

Pre-Heat the stove to high, place heavy pan on stove and apply oil. Get a large bowl and add flour, coconut flour, starch, garlic powder, garlic salt, season salt, and black pepper and give it a quick stir. Dip one at a time marinated chicken that has been socked over night with hot sauce and pineapple juice in a plastic bag into flour. Fry for approximately 15 min, until chicken began to brown and float to the top. Remove chicken from oil give it 7 min to cool and serve hot.

Spaghetti

Ingredients

Spaghetti Pasta Barilla

Lean Fat Ground Beef Roll 5lb

Louisiana Hot links

1 Can of Black Olives

4 Tomatoes

1 Whole garlic

1 Bell Pepper

1 Onion

1 Handful Of Parsley Leaves

¾ Parmesan Cheese

3 Tea Spoons Of Garlic Powder

4 Tea Spoons Of Garlic Salt

3 Tea Spoons Of Season Salt

Directions

Place a large skillet on high heated stove, add ground beef, cut links, bell pepper, garlic, onion, garlic powder, garlic salt, season salt. Let it cook for about 10 min with lid, continuously stir for the rest 5 to 10 min until you no longer see any more pink ground beef. Drain meat, while noodles are boiling add 1 tea spoon of olive oil to prevent sticking to the pot. Cook noodles for approximately 17 min or until pasta is tender but not too soft. Drain noodles, don't rinse. Add noodles and meat together in one large pot, apply diced whole tomatoes, chopped olives, parsley, parmesan cheese, 4 jars of bertolli vineyard marinara sauce, and 1 jar of ragu sauce. Give your spaghetti a quick toss and cook for 10 min, serve hot.

Shrimp and Crab Butini

Ingredients

1 pound of shrimps

Three cheese tortellini butini

½ Country crock butter

Squeeze of soy sauce

2 Jars of creamy alfredo pasta sauce

1 Tea spoon of garlic powder

1 Tea spoon of season salt

1 Tea spoon of garlic salt

Squeeze of teriyaki marinade sauce

1 Bag of crab classic imitation crab

2 Tea spoons of parsley flakes

Directions

Add 4 cups of water to pot, heat stove to high. Cook shrimp butini for about 10 min, after pasta is finish boiling strain the pasta. Place the pasta in pan, 6 inch deep. More than enough room to mix all ingredients. Heat one stick of country crock butter in a separate pot, low heat. Add a squeeze of soy sauce, squeeze of teriyaki marinade sauce. 1 tea spoon of garlic powder, 1 tea spoon of garlic salt, 1 tea spoon of season salt, and 2 tea spoons of parsley flakes. Toss the shrimp into pot, cook for about 3 min until turn pink. Pour the shrimp with all the flavorings in the pot into the 6-inch pan of pasta. Add both jars of creamy alfredo. Bag of imitation crab with parmesan cheese. Toss until completely coated. Serve as desired.

Smoked Turkey and Macaroni

Ingredients

1 bag of penne pasta

2 cups of milk

1 cup of heavy cream

1 stick of I cant believe it not butter

2 cups of pepper jack cheese

2 cups of sharp cheddar cheese

1 tea spoon of season salt

2 tea spoons of garlic salt

2 tea spoons of garlic powder

1 pack of smoked turkey legs

Directions

On a heated stove cooking on high heat, add smoked turkey legs into boiling pot filled with 7 cups of water. Cook for 2 hours with lid. When done turn off heat move pot to a coaling spot. While noodles are boiling in 6 cups of water with 1 tea spoon of salt on high heat with lid for 10 min. When finish, drain noodles. Get another separate boiling pot, add 2 glasses of milk, 1 heavy cream, 2 eggs and boil till thickens. Add to macaroni with a stick of butter, tear off meat add to pot spread over macaroni with cheese on top. Cook for 15 min in oven and serve hot.

Lemon Water

Get 2 cups of water, pour it into a boiling pot until it comes to a boil on high heat. With 1 lemon cut into 4 quarters inserted into pot. When done turn off heat

Wait approximately 5 min before pouring into cup, enjoy the smooth sensation of detoxification. Hot Lemon water is how I start my day every morning, giving me a jump start to whatever sickness gets thrown at me. Also, pushing down unwanted mucus. Soothing and preventing upset stomach aches. A healthy cheap regulation drink. Benefits of cold mornings, with vitamin C for your immune system.

Fruit Oatmeal Bowl

Ingredients

1 Cup of oats

2 Cups of water

1 sliced banana

2 sliced straw berrys

handful of blue berries

Half cup of milk

Directions

Add 2 cups of boiling Water to a medium pot, when water comes to a bowl add in oatmeal and stir continuously until oats are done. Oats take approximately 5 min to cook firmly. Add to bowl. Topped with a banana, handful of berries. 2 straw berry, milk and serve hot.

Scrambled Eggs with Smothered Potatoes

Ingredients

4 Large eggs

½ cup of heavy cream

6 Tablespoons olive oil

4 Medium washed potatoes, diced into ½ quarters

½ onion chapped

½ Green pepper

1/5 Tea spoon ground pepper

1/3 Tea spoons Kosher salt

Directions

Heat skillet medium with oil, when oil is hot place diced potatoes in the pan with onions and bell pepper until lightly golden brown and tender. Whisk eggs together in a medium size bowl, and pour over potatoes onions and bell pepper in heated pan. Cook the eggs until done.

Stuffed Shrimp Omelet

Ingredients

2 pinches of diced onion

2 eggs

2 tea spoons of heavy cream

1/8 tea spoons of salt

1 pinch of pepper

1 Table spoon of butter

1/3 filled in cup of shredded cheese

Handful of diced shrimp

1 pinch of spinach

½ of diced chorizo pork links

Directions

Get a large bowl apply eggs, heavy cream, salt, pepper, onion in a small bowl until blended. Heat butter in 7 to 10-inch nonstick omelet pan or skillet over medium heat. Tilt pan to coat bottom. Pour in all the egg mixture. Mixture should be pour in pot evenly fitting the angles of the whole pot. Tilt cooked portion of the egg from edges toward the center so the uncooked eggs cook properly. Continue to tilt as needed until eggs are no longer running from side to side. Lift omelet with spatula to see if egg is cooked to your standard underneath. When top surface is thicken with no running from the eggs. Apply all the ingredients exactly on one side of the omelet. Fold omelet in half with spactular covering the filling. Flip side to side until it turns brown on each side. Place on plate, serve hot

Fish and Grits Recipe

Ingredients

3/4 Cup of grits

1 tea spoon of I cant believe its not butter

2 pieces of cat fish

Crisco oil

Pinch of paprika

Pinch of salt

pinch of pepper

Pinch of garlic powder

½ of beating egg

3 to 4 tea spoons of heavy cream

1 ¼ cup of Corn Meal

Directions

Add 5 cups of water to a bowling pan, bring it to a boil over high heat. Stir continuously and thoroughly until grits are well mixed. Cover the pot with lid just in case grits start to pop. Then you would lower the temperature and cook for approximately 30 min stirring occasionally. Add more water as needed. You would know if the grits are cooked right if you see a smooth texture throughout stirring it. Add butter, stir in half and leave the remaining on top. In a large bowl add ½ of beaten egg with 3 to 4 tea spoons of heavy cream, pinch of garlic salt, pinch of garlic powder, and a pinch of season salt. To help coating stick to the fish, to give it a thicker crispy texture. On high heat, cooking fish for approximately 15 min until turn brown on each side. Serve hot for best taste.

Fried Cauliflower

Ingredients

1 Bag of cauliflower

Squeeze of heavy cream

3 eggs

1 tea spoon of kosher

Crisco oil

Flour

Bread crumbs

Directions

Combine eggs into bowl with heavy cream and salt, give it a quick stir. In a additional bowl, add 1 cup of corn meal, 1 cup of flower, 1 tea spoon of bread crumbs mixed together. Place cauliflower into egg bowl, toss it for 5 seconds. Dip cauliflower into cornmeal for coating, if not thick enough re-dip into egg and back to cornmeal. Once all of the cauliflower has been coated, begin to fry altogether on high heat until it turns brown or crispy looking. Remove from heat and serve hot.

Cabbage Shrimp Eggrolls

Ingredients

3 Bacon strips

1 pound of shrimps

1 slices of chopped cabbage

1 pack of eggrolls

1 squeeze of soy sauce

1 stick of country crock butter

1 spoon of garlic powder

Pinch of garlic salt

Pinch of season salt

Pinch of cayenne pepper

Crisco oil

Directions

Place two skillets on the stove, one with devein shrimps cooking on medium. In the other pot you have your bacon cooking on high in the skillet for about 5 to 7 min. Fry until bacon is crispy not burnt. Add Crisco oil with chopped cabbage cook for about 8 min, stir until tender. Turn off fire, add a handful of crumbled bacon on top of cabbage. Add 1 stick of butter into the skillet, a squeeze of soy sauce, 1 spoon of garlic powder, pinch of garlic salt. Pinch of season salt, pinch of cayenne pepper. Lastly add devein shrimps. Stir 3 to 4 min, pour shrimps with sauce into cabbage stir. Let it get cool for 10 min then began to wrap. Lay one egg roll out at a time like a diamond, add 2 to 3 table spoons of shrimp and cabbage in the middle of the wrap. Brush egg or flour and water mixed until a paste around the edges. Flip the top part of the arrow over the middle where the food is centered. Flip both of the side pointing at one another. Roll the egg roll till completely sealed. Fry till brown and crisp. Remove, drain and serve hot.

Shrimp Ground Beef, and Jalapeno and Cheese Eggrolls

Ingredients

½ jalapeno

1 pound of ground beef

4 ounces of cheese

Peanut oil

7-inch square egg roll wrapping

1 spoon of salt

Directions

Heat a large skillet on the stove top over medium high heat. Place ground beef into skillet, break apart the ground beef with a spatula. Repeatedly toss and stir until the meat turns brown completely. Add your spoon of kosher salt and stir the ground beef every 3 min until you hit the 12 min mark. Turn off heat from skillet pour meat into a drainer. Drain until grease is removed, pour meat into a large bowl. Lay out one of the eggroll, place 3 to 4 tea spoons of ground beef and cheese onto eggrolls skins lined in the middle. Make sure one end of the corners is pointing towards you. Use egg or flour paste to seal all around for a secure egg roll. Fold top corner over meat and cheese, fold left and right corners towards the center. Keep rolling until the last pointed end is sealed. Repeat with many eggrolls as desired. Add eggrolls into heated high skillet, fry turning eggroll until brown and crispy. Remove from skillet and place onto napkins and serve hot.

Brussel Sprout Salad

Ingredients

1 pound of brussel sprouts

2/3 cranberries

¾ walnuts

1 chopped tomato

1 cup of black beans

pinch of kosher salt

pinch of black pepper

4 ounces of shredded cheese

Directions

Rinse brussels sprouts, cut off all pieces of the stem end. Place brussel sprouts into a food processor or knife into desirable bites. Re-rinse brussel sprouts again to prevent herbicides and pesticides. Place sliced brussels sprouts into a bowl, add dried cranberries, walnuts, tomatoes, black beans, kosher salt, black pepper, cheese.

Fried Broccoli

Ingredients

Pinch of kosher salt

pinch of garlic salt

1 spoon of garlic powder

pinch of black pepper

1 pound of broccoli

2 eggs

1 cup of cornmeal

Directions

Heat pot filled with Crisco oil to high, place egg into bowl. Stir mix spices, black pepper, garlic powder, garlic salt, kosher salt into bowl of stirred eggs. Add broccoli into the bowl toss with hands. Add toss broccoli into pot fry until it turns a light golden brown color up to 10 min. remove and serve hot.

Sweet Potatoes Fries

Ingredients

1 egg

1 cup of cornmeal

pinch of salt

Crisco oil

Directions

Cut the sweet potatoes into sticks 1/3 to ½ inch wide and 4 inches long. Mix the potatoes into the stirred bowl of eggs, toss them. Place egg battered fries into a bag or container filled with cornmeal. Shake until fries are covered well.

On high heat, place fries into pot filled with Crisco oil until fries turn a golden brown and crisp. Flip and cook until you see a golden brown color on the other side. About 10 to 15 min total, remove sweet potatoes fries from pot. Place them on a napkin padded baking sheet and serve hot.

Collard Greens

Ingredients

1 large smoked ham hocks

1 large smoked turkey

1 whole garlic peeled

2 bunches of turnips

2 bunches of collard greens

1 large white onion

1 green bell pepper

1 red bell pepper

1 can of beef broth

7 tea spoons of cayenne pepper

6 tea spoons of paprika

5 tea spoons of garlic powder

5 tea spoons of season salt

Directions

Wash collard greens and turnups in cold water with salt, 15 to 20 cups of water filling the pot to half. Bring your half pot of water to a boil over high flame, add more water if needed. Place your 2 bunches of collards, 2 bunches of turnups and remove stem. Apply large smoked turkey, large smoked ham hocks, whole peeled garlic, large white onion, large green pepper, large red pepper, corn of broth, tea spoon of cayenne pepper. Add 6 tea spoons of paprika, 5 tea spoons of garlic powder, 5 tea spoons of season salt with lid on top of the pot for 3 to 4 hours. When the greens are done turn off the heat and serve.

Fried Carrots

Ingredients

pinch of salt

1 egg

½ cup of bread crumbs

Directions

Rinse carrots, pat dry and grip firmly cutting carrots in the middle. Cut off stem, dip carrots into stirred egg. Toss around, and battered with crumbs. Heat deep frying pan to high. Place fries into pan until you see a light golden brown color, remove from pan. Apply kosher salt and serve hot.

Combination Salad

Ingredients

1 pound of kale

half of diced cabbage

1 cup of walnuts

2 diced avocados

1 diced avocado seed (food processor)

4 inches of aloe vera diced

3 diced tomatoes

handful of cilantro

½ of wheat grass

4 ounce of cheese

5 eggs diced

2 inches of ginger

4 cloves of garlic

squeeze of olive oil

squeeze of ranch

Directions

Cut the kale and cabbage after rinsing, cut from top to bottom. Remove loose ends so only clean compact leaves remain. Position the leaves so the steam end is flat against the cutting board for a safe perfect cut. Slice the cabbage and kale in half from top to bottom create quarters. Place leaves into bowl add walnuts, avocados with diced avocado seed, diced aloe vera, tomato, cilantro, wheat grass, cheese, egg, diced ginger diced garlic, olive oil topped with ranch.

Shrimp and Crab Sandwich

Ingredients

White bolillos fresh baked bread

1 stick of country crock butter

1 pound of cooked deveined shrimp

2/3 cup of mayonnaise

½ olives

I sliced tomato

super lump crab meat in a can

bag of shredded cheese

pinch of kolser salt

pinch of black pepper

1 squeeze of a half lemon

jar of dill slice pickles

2/3 cup of diced onions

squeeze of soy sauce

Directions

Heat stove to medium, add 3 tea spoons of butter into frying pan and add buns. Flip continuously until you see a slight brown toast look. Remove buns, add 1 stick of butter into the same frying pan. Add shrimps, salt, pepper, and a squeeze of soy sauce. Cook for 3 min flip continuously until pink. Turn off heat. Move pot to a cool pilot to prevent from over cooking. glide mayonnaise on buns, split on one half add shrimp. Other half add lettuce, sliced tomato, diced onions, olives, pickles, squeeze of lemon. And get a couple of tea spoons of the flavoring from which the shrimp was cooked in. and sprinkle onto the food on buns to set off flavor.

Crab Salad

Ingredients

Bag of noodles

1 shallot minced onion

4 cups of mayonnaise

½ cup celery

3 tea spoons of kolser salt

2 tea spoons of black pepper

1 green pepper

1 can of diced black olives

super lump crab meat in a can

1 pack of imitation crab meat

1 pound of shrimps

5 tea spoons of garlic powder

4 tea spoons of garlic salt

3 tea spoons of season salt

¾ of chopped pickles in a cup

Directions

While noodles are boiling, working in batches. Add 7 tea spoons of butter into pot cooking on medium. Add peeled and deveined shrimps, 3 cloves of diced garlic, squeeze of half of lemon. Handful of parsley, squeeze soy sauce, 1 tea spoon of garlic powder, 1 tea spoon of season salt. Stir and toss shrimp to combine 4 min then remove. After 10 min of boiling water into a large pot, add a squeeze of olive oil to prevent noodles sticking. Depending on how thick the noodles are, boil anywhere from 8 to 12 min. it's always safe to taste a couple of noodles to see if they are as desired before over or under cooking. When done remove noodles from boiling water. Pour noodles into drainer. Place noodles into a large tray or bowl. Dress the noodles the noodles with 1 diced white onion. Mayonnaise, bell pepper, celery, black olives, pickles, shrimps, season salt, black pepper, garlic powder.

Fruit Salad

Ingredients

Coconut

1 cup of Peach yogurt

handful of blueberries

sprinkle of raspberries

1 cut straw berries

1 diced dragon fruit

Sprinkle of walnuts

half of banana

couple of grapes

1 diced kiwifruit

Directions

Grip your coconut with a towel. Tap with a hammer and turning as needed in a circular motion. Until the shall starts cracking in half. Once coconut is cut into half, place a half cup of yogurt into coconut topped with blue berries, raspberries, straw berries, dragon fruit, walnuts and a half banana, grapes and kiwifruit.

Sade Go Green Juice

Ingredients

2 cups of diced collard greens

2 cups of diced kale

2 sticks of aloe vera

1 cucumber sliced

1 sliced bell pepper

small slice of water melon

4 figs

Directions

Collectively rinse all of your vegetables, collard greens, kale, aloe vera, cucumber, bell pepper, water melon, figs. Place them on a cutting board. Dice into quarters, place 1/3 at a time into juicer. Flowing out into a large jug so that you can catch all your juice. It's important to drink it right after you make it because it loses its nutrients by seconds. Homemade juices are not close to being pasteurized, there for bacteria can grow and cause poisoning to your system.

Carrot Juice

Ingredients

10 sticks of carrots

1 mint leave

1 lemon sliced into 4 quarters

Directions

Wash carrots thoroughly under cold water, brush or stroke with a towel to clean under water for best results. You have a choice to peel the skin off if desired, but its best to leave it on, the more fiber the better. Be sure to cut the carrots into quarters to fit into juicer, followed with jug to catch every healthy beneficial drip. Serve and drink immediately for best health results.

Beets Juice

Ingredients

half glass of ice

1 inch of ginger

1 beet sliced into 4 quarters

Directions

Rinse well under water with a brush to prevent herbicides and pesticides, cut into 4 quarts positioning quarter beets into a juicer. Position glass under the flow of juicer, fill glass with ice if desired and pour the juice into a tall glass and serve immediately. According to studies, beets lower blood pressure, move your bowls of constipation and may cause red urine one or two time after drinking. This healthy beet can be a stainer. Causing unknown energy to progress, preventing deadly diseases such as cancer.

Aloe Vera Juice

Ingredients

1 ½ Glass filled with water

handful of mint leaves

Handful of wheat grass

Handful of ice

10 long branches of aloe vera

Directions

Cut each Aloe Vera stick into 4 quarters, place into blinder with water, ice, mint leaves, wheat grass. Blend on puree for 3 to 4 min, pour into large glass or jug ad drink immediately. Preferably drink early in the morning or before bed.

Water Melon Juice

Ingredients

Water melon

mint leaves

half glass of ice

Directions

Wash the water melon well. Remove dirt, chop the water melon in half, then chop in layers. Juice the flesh and the rind together. Place large jug underneath stream of juicer, because your about to receive a while lot of juice. Be prepared to receive the best juice ever, served on any occasion. Such as during the summer when Its really hot, dinner, mixed with adult drinks, morning nourishment, and bed time cap you name it. In my house my family are natural juice drinkers, we prefer homemade juice. And most of all with any meal. Not just my children love it, but all children love it. There's nothing greater then babies and adults drinking healthy and nourishing there soul and organs all in one.

Apple Juice

Ingredients

3 Apples per cup

half glass of ice

Directions

Wash the outer part of the apple. Pat dry cut from top to bottom. No need to remove seeds since its going into the juicer. Place cup under stream and drink immediately.

Pineapple Juice

Ingredients

1 Pineapple

half glass of ice

Directions

first wash your pineapple, cut the stem of the pineapple. Cut the pine into layers. No need to worry about the rough skin on the outer part. The juicer will take care of that, give you a smooth sensation of living the tropical life. Apply a jug underneath the stream of the juicer, fiber free flowing through giving you life and energy.

Honeydew Melon Ice Cream

Ingredients

1 Honeydew Melon

4 to 5 scoops of vanilla ice cream

1 small glass of milk

1 Glass of ice

Directions

Always cleanses your fruits to prevent herbicides and pesticides. Give it a pat with a towel, slicing from top to bottom, then in layers. No need to dig any seeds out or separating anything. Place into juicer followed behind a large cup or jug catching every stream. Then get a blinder, pour juice into blinder with 4 to 5 large scoops of vanilla ice cream, 1 small glass of milk, and a glass of ice. Preparing for one of the best ice creams served.

Cantaloupe Ice Cream Shake

Ingredients

1 Cantaloupe

1 Apple

A squeeze of honey

Vanilla ice cream

1 small glass of milk

1 glass of ice

Honey

Directions

First and foremost always wash your fruits to prevent herbicides and pesticides. Pat dry with a towel, cutting cantaloupe from top to bottom into layers. Add 1 clean apple, cut into 4 quarters. Place 2 to 3 slices of cantaloupe at a time with 1 slice of apple into juicer repeatedly. Place a jug beneath the stream of the juicer. Add juice to blinder with a squeeze of honey, 5 scoops of vanilla ice cream, 1 small glass of milk, a glass of ice and blind thoroughly.

Party Fruit Basket

Ingredients

1 passion fruit

1 fig

1 mangosteen

1 handful of blue berries

1 rambotan

1 kiwi

10 aloe vera

1 jackfruit

1 Dragon fruit

1 handful of mango

1 beet

Directions

Party baskets in our family means love, fasting or celebration, also bring in the new year with blessing and money. Or just simply enjoying a healthy fruit just because. These healthy alkaline fruits has been known to cure cancer and a number amount of diseases. I'm no doctor and not up for debates, do your research and I guarantee, you will be the next fruit basket lover.

Whole Chicken

Ingredients

Whole chicken

Oven bags

Aluminum foil

E&J brandy liquor

1 whole garlic chopped

1 chopped green bell pepper

4 chopped shallots

Olive oil

Season salt

Garlic Salt

Garlic powder

Cayenne pepper

Paprika

Directions

Place chicken under running water, give it a quick rinse. When finish place chicken on a flat surface such as a cutting board or baking tray. Stab the chicken all over and stuff it with garlic, bell pepper, and shallots. Place chicken into a large oven bag, marinade with E&J brandy liquor overnight. Remove chicken from bag and place on baking tray. Pour olive oil all over chicken, and began to season your bird with season salt, garlic salt, garlic powder, cayenne pepper, and paprika. Cover chicken with another over bag and aluminum foil covering it. Stick chicken into over preheated to 400 degrees F for 2 hours, and prepare for the best tender flavorful chicken ever.

Meatloaf

Ingredients

- 1 pound of ground beef
- 1 small can of tomato paste
- 1 cup of bread crumbs
- 1 tea spoon of brown sugar
- 1 or 2 eggs
- 2 tea spoons of garlic powder
- 1 tea spoon of season salt
- 2 teas spoons of olive oil greased into pan
- 1 tea spoon of garlic salt

Directions

Heat oven to 400F degrees, gather ingredients. Supply a large bowl, collectively combine ground beef, tomato paste, bread crumbs, brown sugar, 1 or 2 eggs, garlic powder, season salt, and garlic salt. Use your two hands, mush it around for one min until all the flavors are mixed. Grease your meatloaf pan, place meat into pan pour any choice of Rague sauce over it. Wrap with foil, bake for 1 ½ hour and serve.

Avocado Sandwich

Ingredients

Pesto

Kraft sandwich spread

Avocado

Onion

Lettuce

Kosher Dill sliced Pickles

Black olives

1 Tomato

Kolser salt

Bagel

Black Pepper

Directions

Collectively gather all ingredients together, cut bagel in the center from top to bottom. Spread avocado on the lower bread. Add sandwich spread on the top portion with pesto. Work in batches by slicing your onion, lettuce, and tomato. Apply all three on the lower portion, add pickles, olives, salt and pepper. Slice bagel in half and serve.

Sade Favorite Breakfast

Ingredients

- 1 sliced apple
- 3 D'Artagnan Applewood smoked bacon
- 1 sliced avocado
- 1 scrambled egg

Directions

Get a large non-stick skillet, apply bacon and position it to cold pan. Turn heat on high cook until bacon starts to shrink and brown on one side, flip and repeat for the other side. In approximately 7 min it should be done. Remove bacon from pan to a napkin padded trey. Use the same pan to cook eggs, but before use get rid of a little of the bacon oil. Cook for about 4 to 6 min total, remove eggs. Place eggs on plate alone with bacon, avocado, and apple. Serve hot.

Fried Lobster

Ingredients

2 Eggs

3 pounds of lobster

Crisco oil

1 ½ cup of cornmeal

1 tea spoon of season salt

1 tea spoon of garlic salt

1 tea spoon of garlic powder

Directions

Get a large skillet, place on medium heat. Apply oil, while waiting on oil to heat. Combine seasons working in batches. Pour seasons into cornmeal, give it a quick stir to blend in a large bowl or use a large bag to shake all together if preferred. If using the bowl, or bag. Place lobster into stirred egg bowl first, then batter lobster for a thicker cruncher coat. Place lobster into oil and fry until lobster is light brown.

Rice Burgers

Ingredients

2 Cups of rice

Half cabbage sliced

Half of white onion sliced

1 tomato sliced

1 Tea spoon of season salt

1 tea spoon of franks red hot original seasonal blend

1 tea spoon of paprika

2 tea spoons of flour

2 handfuls of shredded sharp cheese

1 egg

1 Pack of fold it sweet Hawaii flat bread

Kraft sandwich spread1 Tea spoon of parmesan cheese

Directions

Get a large bowl, add 2 cups of rice. Fresh rice or overnight rice. 2 handfuls of cheese, tea spoon of parmesan cheese, tea spoon of season salt, tea spoon of franks red hot original seasonal blend, tea spoon of paprika, tea spoons of flour, and a egg. Use both hands and press down on ingredients and mush and squeeze for one min, then began to form a patty. Place patties on clean tray for frying. Get a large skillet, heat pilot to medium. Add ¾ of Crisco oil, wait for skillet to get warm. Place patties in skillet to fry, 2 min with each side. Must be a light brown on each side, remove from skillet. Place rice patties on a napkin tray. On a clean plate, lay out flat bread. Add sandwich spread on both sides, place burger patty on one end with sliced tomato, onion cabbage and a sprinkle of shredded cheese. Fold bread over, and enjoy the most multi- friendly rice burgers ever.

Goulash

Ingredients

5 cups of water

3 cups of Rice

1 pound of Ground beef

1 Green bell peppers

1 Red bell peppers

1 yellow bell peppers

1 Tomato paste large

3 garlic cloves

1 tea spoon of accent salt

1 tea spoon of season salt

1 tea spoon of garlic salt

1 tea spoon of garlic power

Directions

In a large pot over medium add 5 cups of water, while that's bowling. Get a large skillet, add ground beef, 8 min into cooking. Drain meat, place back on stove over medium. Add tomato paste and a half cup of water. Green bell pepper, red bell pepper, yellow bell pepper, chopped garlic, accent salt, season salt, garlic salt, garlic powder and stir then cover with a lid. When water comes to a bowl add rice, after approximately 45 min sample rice with a spoon to see if it's as desired. Rinse and drain. After 10 to 15 min ground beef should be brown. Combine cooked rice into ground beef. Stir and serve

Lasagna

Ingredients

2 pounds of ground beef

Lasagna noodles

smoked polish sausages

1 can of black olives

1 8 ounce of shredded sharp cheddar cheese

1 8 ounce of shredded pepper jack cheese

1 8 ounce of shredded mozzarella cheese

Cottage Cheese

1 can of tomato paste

1 jar of Ragu sauce

Barilla pesto sauce

1 onion

1 green bell pepper

half clove of garlic

2 tea spoons of season salt

4 tea spoons of garlic powder

2 tea spoons of garlic salt

Parmesan cheese

Parsley flake

Directions

Get a large pot, add 8 oz of water with 1 tea spoon of salt and a Squeeze of olive oil. Allow water to come to a boil. Add Lasagna noodles with lid. After 8 to 9 min of boiling remove and drain. Add another large skillet, high heat. Apply ground beef, polish sausages, onion, green bell pepper, diced garlic, season salt, garlic powder, garlic salt all together, allow meat to cook approximately 10 min with lid. Drain meat, leave meat in pot, add tomato paste followed with a half cup water and half jar of ragu sauce and stir juicy meat. Get a large baking dish or tray, pour the remaining of ragu sauce in the baking tray first and spread out. Place noodles on top of sauce layered, side by side. Add one 8- ounce bag of mozzarella cheese over noodles, a cup meat and spread out with parmesan cheese, add a little more to fill in spots if needed. Apply another layer of noodles over meat, add one 8 -ounce bag of pepper jack cheese over noodles. Apply a cup of meat over cheese spread out with cottage cheese, more strips of layered noodles with Pesto sauce spread all over followed with parsley flakes, chopped olives and 1 8 -ounce of shredded Sharp Cheddar.

Tofu Burgers

Ingredients

Tofu

Flat Bread

Sliced Lettuce

Sliced onions

Sliced Tomato

Sliced pickles

Shredded Cheese

Sandwich Spread

Olives

Teriyaki sauce

Directions

Place a non-stick skillet on stove, squeeze of olive oil until oil begins to shimmer on medium high. Slice tofu in burger layers, flip front and back in teriyaki sauce. Place in skillet, cook for approximately 5 min on each side then remove from skillet. Add tofu to one side of the flat bread with tomato, onion, pickle, lettuce, cheese, sliced olives and sandwich spread on the opposite side. Fold tofu burger and enjoy hot.

Devil Eggs with Shrimp and Crab

Ingredients

Eggs

Pickle Mayonnaise

Green onions

Shrimp

Boss claw crab meat

Season salt

Garlic Salt

Garlic powder

I cant believe its not butter

Red bell pepper

Soy sauce

Directions

Place pot on the stove, bring water to a boil on high heat. Insert eggs to cook for approximately 20 min. Remove eggs to strainer, run cold water over eggs in the sink. Pill one egg at a time under running water until all are pilled and slice them from top to bottom length wise. Use a small spoon to scoop out yellow yoke to a bowl, apply pickle mayonnaise, green onions, season salt, and garlic powder. Use the same spoon to mix in flavors. Once ingredients are combined, use your spoon to scoop in yolk mixture back into egg. Place fixed eggs to the side in a tray, place small skillet on stove high heat. Add half stick of butter into skillet, once butter is melted. Apply clean devein shrimp, soy sauce, garlic salt, garlic powder. Stir for approximately 4 to 5 min, remove skillet from pilot to prevent from over cooking. Scoop out shrimp with large spoon to collect flavors from butter, place onto of devil egg one at a time until complete. Then apply boss claw crab meat, serve hot.

Steak and Shrimps

Ingredients

Boneless top sirloin steak

1 Pound of Shrimps

Soy sauce

1 Green bell pepper

1 Red bell pepper

1 Garlic

Season Salt

Garlic salt

Garlic powder

Olive oil

Directions

Get a large skillet with 3 tea spoons of oil over high heat, add garlic, red bell pepper, green bell pepper with overnight marinated soy sauce steak. Seasoned on both sides, with season salt, garlic powder, and garlic salt. Flip steak for 5 min on each side to brown before cooking through, then low heat to medium to cook for approximately 1 hour and 40 with foil for medium rare. In an additional skillet, on high heat. Add clean devein shrimp, with one stick of butter, soy sauce, season salt, garlic salt, garlic powder. Cook for approximately 3 to 4 min on high heat, place shrimps on plate with a large spoon for additional flavors from the ingredients from shrimps, with steak on the side and serve hot.

Pasta with Shrimps

Ingredients

Pasta Noodles

shrimps

5 tea spoons of salt

stick of butter

squeeze of soy sauce

garlic powder

garlic salt

red bell pepper

green bell pepper

cilantro

chopped garlic

Directions

Over high heat, bring pot to boil. Add 5 tea spoons of salt. While wait for the pot to come to a boil, in a separate skillet. Add a stick of butter with a squeeze of soy sauce, garlic powder, garlic salt, season salt, red bell pepper, green bell pepper, cilantro, chopped garlic. Cook for approximately 5 min, add clean deveined shrimps. Cook for about 2 min on each side until shrimps turn pink on each side, remove shrimps to boil to prevent from over cooking in hot skillet. Add noodles to boiling pot with a squeeze of olive oil to prevent from sticking. Cook for 15 min, strain the pasta. In an additional large skillet add pasta with bertolli garlic alfredo pasta sauce, half of cup of pasta water from pasta. 1 stick of butter, grated black pepper. Cook for about 5 min until blended, turn off fire. Pour the whole pot of shrimps with ingredients into pasta, give it a quick stir. Add parmesan cheese on top with white shredded cheese and serve.